A Leighton
Organ Album

MUSIC DEPARTMENT

OXFORD
UNIVERSITY PRESS

OXFORD
UNIVERSITY PRESS

Great Clarendon Street, Oxford OX2 6DP, England
198 Madison Avenue, New York, NY10016, USA

Oxford University Press is a department of the University of Oxford.
It furthers the University's aim of excellence in research, scholarship,
and education by publishing worldwide

Oxford is a registered trade mark of Oxford University Press
in the UK and in certain other countries

© Oxford University Press 2002

ISBN 0-19-322292-2 978-0-19-322292-2

Music and text origination by
Barnes Music Engraving Ltd., East Sussex

Contents

FANFARE

KENNETH LEIGHTON

In a moderate march time – very rhythmical

Manual

Gt. *f*

Pedal

OXFORD UNIVERSITY PRESS, MUSIC DEPARTMENT, GREAT CLARENDON STREET, OXFORD OX2 6DP

ROCKINGHAM

KENNETH LEIGHTON

* The tune should be clear but not too predominant.

* A new colour here.

* A new colour here.

TOCCATA ON HANOVER

No. 6 of *Six Fantasies on Hymn Tunes for Organ*, Op. 72

KENNETH LEIGHTON

* The crotchets short, but not too short.

ODE

KENNETH LEIGHTON

To Herrick Bunney

ST COLUMBA (ERIN)

No. 4 of *Six Fantasies on Hymn Tunes for Organ*, Op. 72

KENNETH LEIGHTON

PAEAN

KENNETH LEIGHTON

This work was given its first performance by Simon Preston in the Royal Festival Hall, London, on 25 January 1967 (the 40th anniversary of The Organ Club): he has recorded it on Argo ZRG 528 (stereo) RG 528 (mono). Duration 4½ minutes.

un poco liberamente e con fantasia